For Luke and Lil

A & C Black (Publishers) Limited
35 Bedford Row, London WC1R 4JH

© 1986 Susanna Ray

Filmset by August Filmsetting, Haydock, St. Helens
Printed in Hong Kong by Dai Nippon Printing Co. Limited

Ray, Susanna
    Animals at night.
    1. Nocturnal animals——Juvenile literature
    I. Title
    591 QL755.5
    ISBN 0-7136-2656-9

Animals at Night

Susanna Ray

A & C Black · London

As the sun begins to sink, the shy roe deer
come out of their hiding places in the
woods. They are looking for young grass
shoots to eat.

Hares like to play in the cool of the evening. As it gets darker many birds are settling down to sleep, but the barn owl has just begun its night's hunting.

At dusk small animals, like snails and woodlice, crawl out from under stones. The male crickets begin to sing and this female climbs a grass stem to listen for them.

It's almost dark, so you can see the tiny lights made by glow worms. Hidden in the undergrowth, the nightjar wakes up from her day's rest and begins to sing.

Deep in the woods, the fox goes off to
hunt for food. She leaves her cubs behind.
If an enemy comes too close, the cubs will
run back into their underground home.

The badger family have been sleeping in their underground tunnels all day. Now that it is dark, they come out to collect fresh grass for bedding. They will stay up until dawn, looking for worms and small animals to eat.

Small animals rustle about in the leaves
and moss on the forest floor. The shrew
has found an earthworm and the
woodmouse is looking for berries.

The frog and the pipistrelle bat are catching their dinner. They snap up mosquitoes which have hatched from the water.

The tawny owl perches high in a tree.
It has caught a mouse in its sharp talons.
When dawn comes the owl will go back to
its roost and sleep.

The nightingale begins to sing long
before dawn, while most of the other birds
are still asleep.

At dawn, a family of hedgehogs are ready to curl up and sleep in their nests. They have been busy hunting all night.

In the early morning, the rabbits are still out in the fields. They have spent the night feeding and will soon go back to their burrows.

The badgers, the owls and many other animals are already fast asleep in their homes. But the daytime animals, like us, are just waking up.

This page will tell you more about the animals which you might find at night. Some of these animals, like the frog, are awake during the day but often hunt at night. Other animals, like the badgers, sleep during the day and only come out at night. They are called *nocturnal animals.* Nocturnal animals often have poor eyesight but sharp hearing and a good sense of smell.

You're most likely to see roe deer in the evening when they come out to feed. During the day they hide in sheltered places. The males (1) are called bucks and the females (2) are called does. They usually stay in pairs but when they are feeding on open ground, they sometimes stay in small groups for safety. Roe deer use their excellent sight, hearing and smell to help them sense danger. When frightened, they give an alarm bark like a dog's and run for cover.

During the day, the brown hare (1) rests in a hollow in the long grass, called a form. Hares like to live on open ground and they are most active in the evening. The bucks (males) box and chase each other to attract the does (females). They feed on grasses, clover (2), dandelions (3), bark, grain and roots.

The barn owl (4) is nocturnal. It begins to hunt for small animals just as the rooks (5) are settling in trees to roost (sleep).

The snail (1) spends the day in a dark damp place, coiled up inside its shell. If it came out into the sunshine, its body might dry up. The woodlouse (2) hides under a stone or inside tree bark. At night, when the air is cool and damp, these animals come out to feed.

On warm evenings the male great green bush crickets rub their front wings together to make a 'singing' noise which attracts the females (3). At night many flowers, like the buttercup (4), close their petals.

During the day, the nightjar (1) nests in gorse or bracken, in woodland clearings or on commons. Its dull brown colour helps it to blend in with its surroundings, but at night you might hear its 'churring' song. The nightjar eats beetles and hawkmoths.

On summer evenings the female glow worms (2) climb grass stems and give off a bright light from their abdomens. The male glow worms, which look like beetles, are attracted by the light.

The fox (1) and her cubs spend most of the day in the 'earth', a tunnel underground. Often they live in tunnels left by badgers. Foxes have a very good sense of smell, keen hearing and good night sight. They stalk and catch animals such as mice, rats, small birds and poultry. The long-eared bat (2) can't see very well. Like all bats, it uses its ears instead of its eyes. It sends out a high pitched squeaking noise. If anything is nearby, the bat hears an echo. This sound guides the bat as it hunts for insects to eat.

The badgers' underground home is called a sett. It has many tunnels with rooms, or chambers, which are lined with dry plants for sleeping on. Badgers are very clean animals. They change their bedding frequently and dig special latrines away from the sett. Badgers use their keen sense of smell and sharp hearing to find food.

The garden tiger moth (1) only flies at night. During the day it rests on a tree trunk. Like all moths, it is attracted to light.

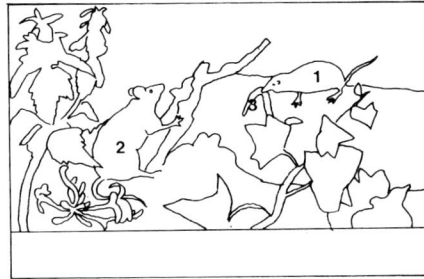

The common shrew (1) and the woodmouse (2) have many enemies so they usually come out only at night. The shrew must eat $\frac{3}{4}$ of its own weight of food every night. It uses its long snout to turn over dead leaves and surface soil for food such as earthworms.

The woodmouse is a good climber, jumper and swimmer. It digs a burrow underground to store food such as acorns, nuts, grain and fruit for winter.

The common frog (1) sits among the yellow flag irises (2) and the bullrushes (3) at the edge of the water. During the day it usually stays in a cool damp place, or in the water. Frogs catch insects on the end of their long sticky tongues. This one is waiting to catch the mosquitoes (4) which have hatched that evening from mosquito larvae in the water. The tiny pipistrelle bat (5) sleeps in tree holes or under eaves during the day. Often, large colonies of these bats sleep together. At night they hunt for insects.

In daylight, the tawny owl (1) roosts (sleeps) in hollow trees, or in barns. Its large eyes and keen hearing help it to hunt for small animals at night. The owl pounces on its prey and grips the animal with its sharp talons. The tawny owl can fly without making any noise, but you might hear its quavering hoot. The nightingale (2) is a summer visitor. In winter, it flies to Africa. The bird's dull brown colour makes it difficult to spot when it is hiding in bushes and trees during the day.

Hedgehogs eat insects, slugs, snails, earthworms, acorns and berries. They have poor eyesight but a good sense of smell so they walk along with their noses close to the ground, sniffing for things to eat. They sleep under hedgerows in nests of leaves and grass. If attacked, they roll up into a prickly ball.

The elephant hawkmoth (1) feeds by sucking nectar from honey-suckle and other flowers which keep their petals open at night.

Rabbits are most active at night, but in quiet places they will come out during the day to feed on grasses and other plants. The best time to look for them is in the early morning or evening. Large numbers of rabbits live together in underground tunnels, called warrens. Look out for rabbit droppings (1) near a warren.

Early in the morning the ground is sometimes wet, even though it hasn't rained. This water on the ground is called dew.